P9-CDA-980

MARY EMMERLING'S

AMERICAN COUNTRY GARDENS

MARY EMMERLING'S

AMERICAN COUNTRY GARDENS

PHOTOGRAPHS BY JOSHUA GREENE

Clarkson Potter/Publishers
New York

Published by Clarkson N. Potter, Inc., 201 East 50th Street, New York, New York 10022. Member of the Crown Publishing Group.

CLARKSON POTTER, POTTER, and colophon are trademarks of Clarkson N. Potter, Inc.

Manufactured in Japan

Design by Howard Klein and Jane Treuhaft

Library of Congress Cataloging-in-Publication Data
Emmerling, Mary Ellisor. [American country gardens]
Mary Emmerling's American country gardens /
photographs by Joshua Greene.—1st ed.
1. Gardens—Gift books. 2. Gardens—United States—Gift books. 3. Country life—Gift books. 4. Country life—United States—Gift books. I. Greene, Joshua. II. Title. III. Title: American country gardens.
SB450.98.E47 1991 90-48762
712′.6—dc20 CIP
ISBN 0-517-58364-X
10 9 8 7 6 5 4 3 2 1
First Edition

To all my friends who love gardening,
but especially Beverly Jacomini

—M.E.

To Joe Eula, who has taught me that the
simplicity in nature is the essence of
a passionate life

—J.G.

Gardens have existed since the beginning of history, and despite the toil they require, they have always been associated with pleasure. From Eden to the Hanging Gardens of Babylon to our own backyards, gardens have been the closest thing to paradise that can be achieved on earth. Here lovers have had their trysts, poets their greatest thoughts, and busy men and women a moment or two of peace. ☆ *My grandmother Marthena Williams gave me one of the best presents of my life—a love of gardens. In the rose garden behind her town house (one of the best collections of roses in Washington, D.C.), she served her grandchildren gingersnaps and lemonade and told us romantic stories of her childhood. Her grandfather was President*

Benjamin Harrison, and the tales were always good ones, but the garden—with its heavy scent of roses, the buzzing of bumblebees, a tapestry of colors, and the heat of a Georgetown summer day—often upstaged the storytelling. In my grandmother's garden I learned the pleasure of daydreaming on long, tranquil afternoons. ☆ *Since then, I have always cultivated a garden of my own whenever I can, and I have enjoyed seeing all of the different kinds of gardens people have created across the country. City gardens are rare treasures, but I think that country gardens have the most personality. As the link between the house and the wilder fields and forests beyond, the country garden often becomes an outdoor room, enclosed by fences and furnished with benches and folk art. These*

touches of individuality give each garden the stamp of its owners—comfort, drama, even a sense of humor. ✯ *All gardens require toil, but an hour spent turning the earth or watering tender seedlings always rewards the gardener with many hours of enjoyment later. Gardeners learn to cooperate with Nature to create a feast for the senses—attracting butterflies with fragrant flowers and songbirds with handsome houses made just for them. The splashing of water from a fountain or a nearby brook adds a backdrop of sound more pleasing than a symphony; the array of reds, yellows, and blues of the border garden is a dazzling sight; and the harvest from the vegetable garden at summer's end gives us the most delicious meals of the year.* ☆ *This book is a tribute to all of the wonderful gardens I have known—and to your garden pleasures, too. Every summer evening when the weather is fine, we have our supper outdoors, surrounded by herbs and flowers, under blue sky and then stars. In the winter, we look longingly through frosted windows at chairs heaped with snow, waiting for the season to turn*

and bring back the garden again. Whether your garden blooms for two months a year or for ten, whether it skirts a country cottage or a city lot, I hope you enjoy our American Country Gardens.

Happy gardening!

Mary Emmerling

And 'tis my faith that every flower
Enjoys the air it breathes.

WILLIAM WORDSWORTH

See how the flowers, as at parade,
Under their colours stand displayed:
Each regiment in order grows,
That of the tulip, pink, and rose.

ANDREW MARVELL

Genius will thrive without training, but it does not the less reward the watering pot and pruning knife.

MARGARET FULLER

If I could put my words in song
And tell what's there enjoyed,
All men would to my gardens throng,
And leave the cities void.

RALPH WALDO EMERSON

The Admiral says that he never beheld so fair a thing: trees all along the river, beautiful and green, and different from ours, with flowers and fruits each according to their kind, many birds and little birds which sing very sweetly.

CHRISTOPHER COLUMBUS

Where'er you walk, cool gales shall fan the glade,
Trees, where you sit, shall crowd into a shade:
Where'er you tread, the blushing flow'rs shall rise,
And all things flourish where you turn your eyes.

ALEXANDER POPE

Again rejoicing Nature sees
Her robe assume its vernal hues,
Her leafy locks wave in the breeze,
All freshly steep'd in morning dews.

ROBERT BURNS

Which May had painted
with his softe showers
This garden full of leaves
and of flowers.

GEOFFREY CHAUCER

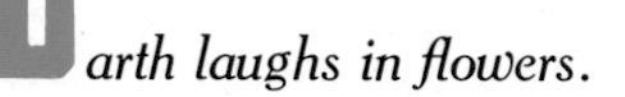

Earth laughs in flowers.

RALPH WALDO EMERSON

HERBS
BAY

How could such sweet and wholesome hours
Be reckoned but with herbs and flowers?

ANDREW MARVELL

My garden, with its silence and the pulses of fragrance that come and go on the airy undulations, affects me like sweet music. Care stops at the gates, and gazes at me wistfully through the bars.

ALEXANDER SMITH

In wit, as in nature, what affects our hearts
Is not th' exactness of particular parts;
'Tis not a lip or eye we beauty call,
But the joint force and full result of it all.

ALEXANDER POPE

Before green apples blush,
Before green nuts embrown,
Why, one day in the country
Is worth a month in town.

CHRISTINA ROSSETTI

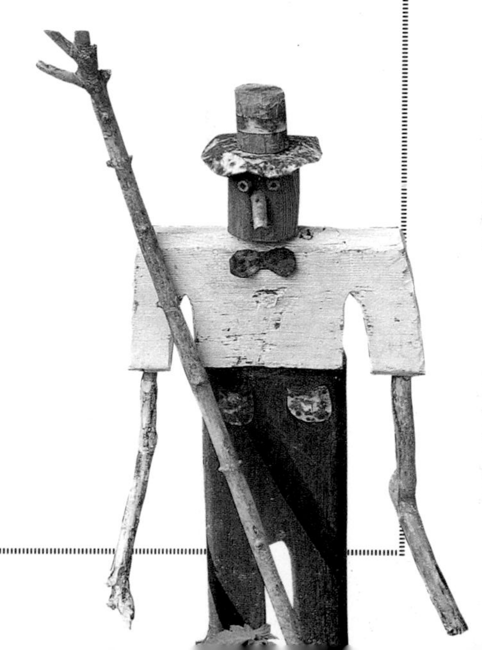

I know a little garden close,
Set thick with lily and red rose,
Where I would wander if I might
From dewy morn to dewy night.

WILLIAM MORRIS

The windflower and the violet, they perished long ago,
And the brier-rose and the orchid died amid the summer glow;
But on the hill the golden-rod, and the aster in the wood,
And the yellow sunflower by the brook, in autumn beauty stood.

WILLIAM CULLEN BRYANT

Earth is here so kind,
that just tickle her with a hoe
and she laughs with a harvest.

DOUGLAS JERROLD

GARDEN

Show me your garden
and I shall tell you what you are.

ALFRED AUSTIN

A rose, as fair as ever saw the north,
Grew in a little garden all alone;
A sweeter flower did nature ne'er put forth,
Nor fairer garden yet was never known.

WILLIAM BROWNE

How doth the little busy bee
Improve each shining hour,
And gather honey all the day
From every opening flower!

ISAAC WATTS

HERBS

I look upon the pleasure which we take in a garden, as one of the most innocent delights in human life.

JOSEPH ADDISON

TOOLS

Flowers are lovely; love is flower-like;
Friendship is a sheltering tree.

SAMUEL TAYLOR COLERIDGE

Love of trees and plants is safe. You do not run risk in your affections. They are my children, silent and beautiful, untouched by any passion, unpolluted by evil tempers.

ALEXANDER SMITH

To see a world in a grain of sand
And a heaven in a wild flower,
Hold infinity in the palm of your hand
And eternity in an hour.

WILLIAM BLAKE

Rose, thou art the sweetest flower
That ever drank the amber shower;
Rose, thou art the fondest child
Of dimpled Spring, the wood-nymph wild.

THOMAS MOORE

*To sit in the shade on a fine day
and look upon verdure is
the most perfect refreshment.*

JANE AUSTEN

The world puts on its robes of glory now;
The very flowers are tinged with deeper dyes;
The waves are bluer, and the angels pitch
Their shining tents along the sunset skies.

ALBERT LAIGHTON

Beneath the crisp and wintry carpet hid
A million buds but stay their blossoming;
And trustful birds have built their nests amid
The shuddering boughs, and only wait to sing
Till one soft shower from the south shall bid,
And hither tempt the pilgrim steps of Spring.

ROBERT BRIDGES

ACKNOWLEDGMENTS

Doug Cramer

Jimmie Cramer

Dean Johnson

Audrey Julian

Marston Luce

Julie Southworth

Polly Yuhas

With special thanks
to Joshua Greene

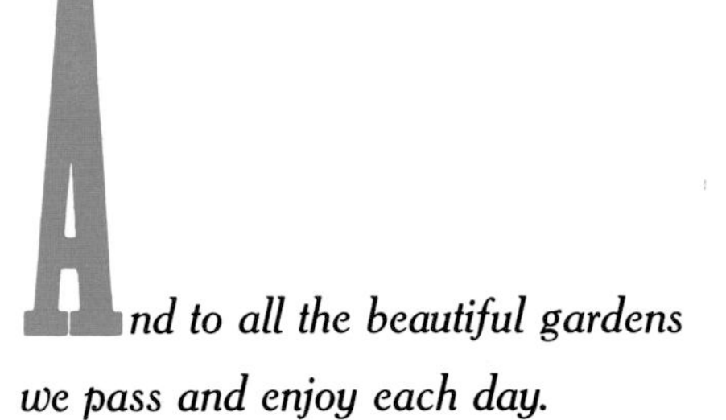

And to all the beautiful gardens
we pass and enjoy each day.